ZEEBA

PATIENT, PERSISTENT PURSUIT

After the Rain
Publishing LLC

SHEILA Y. SCHROEDER

ZEEBA: PATIENT, PERSISTENT PURSUIT

Milton-Freewater, Oregon
Library of Congress Control Number: 2018935774

S he darted out from behind a short stack of bricks by our shed and pranced in a large circle around me. Her zebra-like stripes wrapped her small frame and spilled over her forehead. She was beautiful and her bouncy, charming personality was on full display. We were instantly captivated with each other and my routine trip to the garden exploded with delight.

My voice found a high range of soprano as I cooed, "Here, kitty, kitty." I continued as if she could understand every word. "You are so adorable. Where did you come from? Come here, little sweetie. I want to hold you. Will you let me pick you up?" She lifted her tail as if I were petting her, rubbed up against anything she could find, and padded the earth with her tiny, perfect paws. I imagined she was purring. It seemed that every bone in her body wanted desperately to come to me, but whenever I stepped in her direction, she cautiously withdrew. When I stood still, she resumed her padding and rubbing as if my words were caressing her beautiful furry body.

I glanced around and noticed a large gray cat sitting close to a car trailer parked about ten feet away. She appeared to be assessing the situation with no signs of stress. *It must be the mother of this little bundle of love.* Just then, another small head appeared beside mama. This little one was pure black with big intense eyes that broadcast fear. Those eyes intently followed the sanguine princess who had come to greet me.

3

"So, little sweetie. It looks like you have a mama and a brother or sister."

I moved gingerly to a grassy spot in the field closer to the little family and sat down. Little black kitty disappeared behind the wheel but mama cat didn't budge. I sat down as I continued talking to my newfound friend.

"Come, little one. I won't hurt you. Is this your mommy over here? Come here, sweetie."

She confirmed my assumption by running playfully over to mom and lovingly rubbing against her. Her mother slapped her away and dashed off with black kitty close behind.

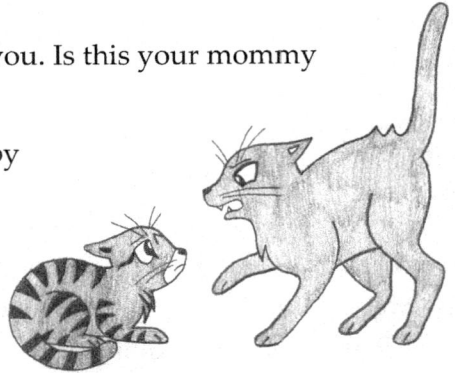

"Oh, honey," I gasped to the stoic little face staring at me. "I'm so sorry, precious. You don't deserve that. Come here, let me hold you and love you. I would never treat you like that." She simply turned her head and began licking her shoulder. Even the cruel rejection by her own mother was not enough to tempt her to trust me.

I wished so much she could talk. I was full of questions. "How did you get here? Where are you staying? How are you surviving? Is your mommy always that mean to you? Does she take care of you or do you have to fend for yourself? Will I ever see you again?"

The barrage of questions must have overwhelmed her, and she scampered off in the direction of a small skiff our neighbor had parked in the field. Effortlessly, she jumped up on the side, poked her nose under the tarp cover, and vanished. *Maybe she is showing me where they live.* I was frightened by the realization that our field, that sidelined a very busy street, might be their home.

Our garden was situated behind our rental house about a mile from where we lived. The shed was attached to a shop and various

4

vehicles and equipment were stored behind it in the open field. They could provide some shelter for this little family, but I couldn't help wondering how long they would last. *If they do live here, where do they get food?* I decided to call our renter to see if she had seen them around. *Maybe she's been feeding them.*

She sighed, "They seem to be living in your shed. But I see them in the neighbor's field occasionally." She continued emphatically, "I don't want to feed three cats."

"I understand. I certainly don't expect you to. I will make sure they are fed if they continue to live here."

After putting my garden tools away, I hurried home to get some kitty food. I pulled into the driveway—and pulled right back out. *What am I thinking? I don't have any food for kittens!* Off to the store I went to purchase some proper food. I grabbed a couple of bowls for food and water.

The sun was painting the horizon as I headed back to the garden. Orange light cascaded behind the treeless mountain just as I pulled into the property.

"Here kitty, kitty. Here's some yummy food for you. Where are you, little sweetie? Aren't you hungry?" No response. I walked to the door and called again while banging the food dish, hoping to attract attention. Nothing.

The silence was painful as I filled the water and food bowls and placed them on the dirt floor inside the shed. *Where is my little furry family?*

"Here, kitty, kitty," I called with decreasing energy. Soon the wannabe hero in me decided to give up and go home. *I'll try again tomorrow.*

Sliding into the driver's seat triggered a flood of memories and mixed emotions from a few weeks before. It all started with a frantic phone call from my husband Jeff.

~~~

I glanced at the cell phone dancing on the counter and picked it up. Jeff interrupted my hello. "Sheila, I'm over at the rental." He sounded out of breath. "I just found two kittens in our shop. They're just days old."

"Honey—slow down. I can barely understand you."

"I don't think they're going to make it. It looks like they've been abandoned."

"Oh no! Where are they?"

"I put them on the seat in the pickup. I'm afraid it's too late. One may already be dead."

It took less than a second for me to land in the driver's seat of my car and not much longer to drive the mile to our garden. I screeched to a stop beside the pickup door and didn't wait for the cloud of dust to catch up to me. I flung open the pickup door and gasped. They were so tiny and lifeless! I couldn't breathe as I scooped them up in my arms and sped home. My mind was racing ahead of the car, searching my kitchen. *Milk. I need milk. Would they drink milk? All I have is soy milk. Oh no—will that work?*

Neither one moved as I raced inside. The tongue on the tiny lifeless one was hanging out, white and parched. *Of course! They're dehydrated! Liquid. They need liquid—now! Where's that mini-bottle feeder? Oh dear! Did I give that away? What am I going to do? I need something to lay them on. Here's a towel.* I placed it on the table and gingerly laid them down. Still not one sound or movement. "Be strong, little ones. You can do it. Hang on! I'm here to help. Don't give up. Please don't give up!"

I bunched up the towel to form a cradle around the kittens. One tiny black paw moved. *Yes! There's hope! Lord, please let them live. Please help me help them!*

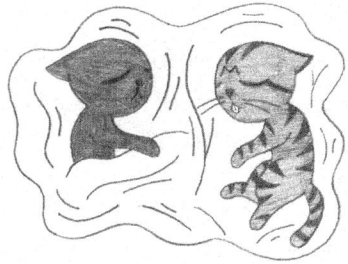

I'll try water first. Dipping my pinky finger in a bowl of water, I cradled the baby's head and dripped some on her dry tongue. I kept praying and dripping more water. Finally, enough liquid gathered in her throat and she miraculously swallowed. *Thank you, God!* More water, more swallows, and then she moved. Oh so slightly, but she moved! *It's working! Hallelujah!* Her mouth closed with one more swallow and she seemed to be resting. *Poor little thing. Just swallowing is hard work for you. I'll let you rest for a bit, sweetie.*

My attention turned to her black brother. Dipping my finger in the water, I touched his lips. That was a big mistake. "Meow, meow, meow," he loudly protested. The more I tried to give him water, the more he resisted. It was obvious that water wasn't going to cut it for him. His little feet and head began moving in search of mommy's milk. *I know, sweetie. I wish your mommy were here too!*

It was time for plan B. *What do I do now?* Instantly, the thought came to me to try canned milk. *Of course! Oh, please help me find a can!* I flung open the doors to the pantry and scanned the shelves. No canned milk in sight. *Oh no. Don't tell me I don't have any.* Frantically, I glanced over the cans again and pushed some soup cans aside. Miraculously, there was one lonely can in the back of the cupboard. *Thank you, Lord. It's not just sparrows you care about; little kittens are important to you too. Thank you. Thank you!*

Black kitty was making enough noise for both of them, but I couldn't mistake a faint new cry coming from the table top. I was thrilled. *The black one must have pushed or scratched his sister and woke her up in his vigorous attempt to find mom.*

It took forever to find the can opener and punch a hole in the top of the can. *I bet this is too rich for them. Maybe I should mix it with a little water—and warm it a little too.*

The table top meows were both comforting and disturbing. I was so thankful they were alive, but their cries accentuated my helpless feeling. *How do mothers of twins deal with two hungry babies at once?*

I soon discovered the task was even more daunting than I thought. They were starved and very impatient. Drop by drop was painfully inadequate and exasperating to them—and to me. I remembered a tiny spoon I had and tried using it. I could get a little more in their hungry mouths, but they started sputtering and coughing. Tears were threatening to flow faster than the milk. *Lord, I need help. I can't do this.* The thought came, *Call Jeff.*

"Honey, I need help," I tearfully pleaded. "Nothing is working. I need some miniature bottles. Please, can you run to the pet store and get some for me?" He could hear the meowing duet in the background and agreed to go right away. "Thank you. Thank you! Please hurry!"

I continued to do what I could, but by the time he walked in the door, all three of us were beyond stressed. He had purchased two bottles, one large one and one small one. "That's all they had," he explained.

The small bottle was a challenge but eventually worked. One of the most satisfying moments of my life was when both baby kittens had full tummies and decided to get some rest. I was exhausted and overjoyed.

"Honey, I can't thank you enough for coming to our rescue."

"Sheila, you know we need to take them back to their mom, don't you?" His words stunned me, the forced reality check unwelcome. My panic returned.

"I can't do that. You said yourself it looked like they were abandoned. I can't take them back there to die!" Tears came again.

"They need their mom, Sheila. They will require around-the-clock care. They'll be hungry again soon and this will start all over again. Besides, this milk is not what's best for them." He was right and I knew it. If their mother was somewhere around, that would be ideal.

"Here's what I think happened," Jeff offered. "The kittens must have been born in the shop, but when I was over there a couple of days ago, I shut the door between the shop and the shed. My guess is that mama cat got shut out and couldn't get back to her kittens." It sounded like a viable explanation, but I was in no mood to risk taking them back.

"I don't know if there even *is* a mama cat. What if she got killed?" My hands began to tremble as I spoke. "What if she *did* abandon them? How can I take them back? They are so helpless!" Jeff finally agreed to go over and see if he could find mama cat.

After he left, I called the renter back. She could tell I was distraught. She assured me mama cat was nearby and agreed that it was best to bring the kittens back and see if their mom would claim them. "Sheila, I'll go out and look too," she offered.

I could feel my stomach relax a bit.

Minutes later the phone rang. Mama cat had been spotted. I found a little box and tenderly put the babies in it. They started crying again, but I knew I was running out of time. Soon it would be dark. I tried to be positive. *It's a good thing they are meowing, Sheila. Then their mom will hear them and come get them.* I drove back to the garden

and lovingly placed the little box in the shed. It was difficult to leave but I knew their mom would never come if I stayed.

Jeff and the renter were talking in the garden. "Honey, it's going to be OK," Jeff assured me. I knew he was trying to comfort me but neither of them seemed to grasp the gravity of the situation. I waited as many minutes as my fearful heart would allow and then hurried back to the shed to check on them. They were still crying and there was no sign of their mom. Back out to the garden I went to plead with Jeff to let me take them back home.

"Give her more time, Sheila. It's what's best for them." The waiting was painful and darkness was settling in. When the renter disappeared inside her house, I ran to check on the kittens.

I noticed right away that the meowing had stopped. *Mama cat must have come after all.* I bent over the box and sure enough, the little black one was gone. I hurried back out, hoping I hadn't interfered with the reclaiming process. *Lord, please help her come back for the tiny one. Help them survive somehow.*

I had to admit Jeff was right and that this had been the best plan. I just knew that in a few minutes I would go back in and the box would be empty. I felt comforted just thinking about them being with their own mother and getting the nourishment they needed. I was hopeful and waited more patiently.

"It's getting dark so fast! There's no light in the shed—I'm afraid I won't be able to see," I murmured half-aloud to Jeff.

"I'll look for a flashlight in the pickup."

The dim light traced my steps to the box—and there she lay, sleeping. I felt sick.

"I'm so afraid the mama has rejected her. Please let me take her home."

"Hon. I know you are worried. I know you want to care for her, but I don't think that is the best thing to do. Please—just leave her tonight. I'm sure mama cat will come and get her."

"I'll never forgive you if something happens to her," I whined.

Against my better judgment and bleeding heart, I drove home. All I could do was cry and pray for a miracle. It took me hours to fall asleep, and I didn't sleep long. At the first hint of dawn, I raced back to the shed. Fumbling to unlock the door and hurrying to the box, I was horrified to find the baby kitten still there. *That does it. I don't care what anybody says. I am taking you home!*

I scooped her up in my arms and held her close. Her little body felt cold and she didn't move. I prayed all the way home. "Lord, please help her. Give her the strength to live." All I could think about was that she had gone another night with no food and no other bodies to keep her warm or comfort her. I felt my jaw clench with anger toward mama cat for taking one baby and leaving the other, toward Jeff for insisting I leave the baby there, and toward myself for not following my heart.

I touched the warm nipple to her lips and cried with relief as her tiny mouth began to suck. She was so weak that she could drink only a few drops at a time. I kept waking her and trying to feed her throughout the day and night. By morning she was much stronger and I was the exhausted one. Jeff was right about the constant care required!

Patiently, I fed her and rubbed her little body gently to help her relieve herself, as mama cat would. It wasn't a fun part of caring for her, but it was necessary. It reminded me that choosing to love and care for someone means choosing to accept the bad with the good.

The first time she purred, my heart could not contain the joy. It was such a precious moment. "Oh, little one, I want to hold you forever!

I wish you could always stay tiny." She contentedly sucked on my pinky finger and purred as she kneaded my arm. "I'm sorry you don't have your real mommy to comfort you and care for you, but I'm thrilled your Creator allowed me to be His provision for you. I am so thankful for the time I get to spend with you."

Often, throughout the day, I would thank God for saving her life and for letting me care for her. I hated having to leave and always hurried home to check on her. Fear gripped me when I thought about two upcoming vacations we had planned long ago. *What am I going to do with this little bundle of love? Who will care for her?* I thought about my sister who loves cats. But I quickly scratched that idea because she worked full time and wouldn't be able to care for her during the day. *Lord, I can't cancel the vacations without wasting a lot of money. Jeff would not be happy about that at all! Please help me find someone who can care for this precious little one.*

The next afternoon I shared my dilemma with a friend. Her face lit up and she blurted out, "Sheila! My daughter gets out of school for the summer next Monday, and she'd *love* to take care of her."

My face lit up. "That would be so awesome—a real answer to prayer!" I went on to explain that it would be at least three weeks because of both trips we had planned, but it didn't seem to faze her.

"I'll talk to Zaonna tonight and see what she says." She gathered her things to leave.

"That would be fantastic. I'd be so relieved," I said as we hugged good-bye.

The unspeakable joy of knowing God deeply cares about the details of my life washed over me. His provision for my need was love in action—tangible evidence I could touch. "Thank you, God, for caring, for loving, for providing. I love you."

Basking in the feeling of being loved and cared for was short-lived. The thoughts of leaving my little friend threatened to overshadow my joy. I began to fret. *Will Zaonna care for her as much as I do? Will she love her and hold her and enjoy her as much as I do? Will she be patient with her and responsible for taking care of all her needs, not just the fun things? She's a teenager with all kinds of distractions. What if she forgets about her and doesn't feed her?*

All this fretting wasn't helpful at all. I reminded myself that worrying is turning to God and saying, "You go ahead and take a break. I got this handled." *No—that is the opposite of what I desire, Lord. I give this little one and this situation back to you. You are far more capable than I am, and your plan is perfect. You have proven that over and over. I refuse to worry one more minute.*

Besides, I didn't know if Zaonna even wanted to take care of her yet. I decided to wait and see. If she agreed, I could talk to her then and get a better idea of how responsible she was going to be.

Zaonna and her mom came over to talk about caring for the little one. As I interacted with Zaonna, I knew my stewing had been in vain and God had provided the perfect answer to my prayer. Zaonna instantly fell in love with baby kitty and held her just as I had. She fed her and we talked about her little routines and the full-time care she required. Her excitement quieted my anxiety and made the thought of leaving on vacation more bearable.

Zaonna smiled at the sleeping baby and asked, "What are you going to name her?"

"I've been thinking about that. I love her zebra stripes. What do you think of the name Zeebe?" We all laughed. But we couldn't think of anything we liked better. "I guess it's settled then," I announced. "We'll call her Zeebe."

It was difficult leaving for vacation, but every time I called to check on Zeebe, Zaonna assured my anxious heart that everything was fine. "Are her eyes open yet? Is she still eating good? Is she sleeping long between feedings? How often do you have to get up in the night?"

"Oh, Sheila. Yes! She finally opened her eyes! And they are beautiful. She is even more adorable now!" The genuine enthusiasm in her voice was comforting. *That's just like God to provide even more than I asked. Not only was she taking great care of Zeebe, but she dearly loved her as well.*

Three weeks flew by and I couldn't wait to get back. But all was not well at home. Someone's heart was breaking. Zaonna had fallen in love with Zeebe and she was having a tough time thinking about giving her up when I returned.

As soon as I arrived home, I called. "Is now a good time to come over and get her?" I asked excitedly. Zaonna attempted to assure me that it was, but I detected hesitation in her voice. "Sure—you can come visit her ... but ... do you have to take her today?"

One look at Zaonna's face when she opened the door confirmed my suspicion. She tried to hide her sadness with a cheerful greeting and a hug, but her demeanor gave away her reluctance. My heart understood; this little one had instantly attached herself to Zaonna's heart too.

I couldn't believe how much she had grown. And her eyes were amazing. Zeebe was looking more and more like a healthy kitten on her way to joining the prestigious cat population. I gingerly reached for her and planted kisses on her tiny head and held her close. Her purring was instant and her eyes were big and beautiful. I wondered if she recognized my smell or if I had been totally replaced. I chose to think she could never forget the one who rescued her.

A battle raged inside me. Every fiber of my body longed to gather up her things and take her home right then. But I also cared about Zaonna and her conflicted heart. *Sheila, you can wait one more night. Leaving her a bit longer might soften the transition. It's the right thing to do, and you could use a good night's rest anyway to recuperate from traveling.*

Late the next morning the phone rang. The caller ID informed me it was Zaonna's mom, Doronna.

"Sheila, I'm worried about Zaonna. She's not doing well."

"Is she sick? Or is this about Zeebe?"

"Definitely Zeebe." The big sigh punctuated her struggle. "She's having a very hard time thinking about giving Zeebe up."

"I totally understand. You can't care for something so tiny and so adorable 24/7 and not fall totally in love with her!"

"I believe taking care of her has awakened all Zaonna's motherly instincts and I'm proud of her for taking such good care of her."

"And it has been such a blessing to know that she was so loved and cared for while I was gone. I'm so thankful."

"Sheila, would you ever consider letting us keep Zeebe? You could come visit *any* time. I promise we'd take excellent care of her. Zjé and I have fallen in love with her too. She's part of our family."

My heart was in my throat. It wasn't hard to empathize with Zaonna; I knew the longing and the tears—how devastating it was to lose something so tiny and so precious. However, I loved this little one too! How powerful feelings can be for something so small and helpless!

"I have such mixed emotions, Doronna. It's tough for me to think about life without little Zeebe now. But if I can feel this attached after one week of caring for her, I imagine Zaonna would feel even more strongly after three weeks of care. And perhaps it might be traumatizing for Zeebe to go back and forth from one mom to another."

"What are you going to do with her while you're working?"

"Well, thankfully, I'm not ever gone too many hours at a time. But you're right—she wouldn't have the constant care that Zaonna could give her."

"It's fun for me to see how well she cares for her. She is truly dedicated."

"I'm so thankful for such an amazing answer to my prayer for someone to care for her. I'm incredibly grateful to you for allowing Zaonna to do that. Let me talk with Jeff and I'll get back to you."

After talking with my practical husband, my heart began to accept—barely—the possibility of giving up my role as mom and becoming grandma to Zeebe instead. I decided to let Zaonna have Zeebe, provided I was given non-negotiable visiting rights whenever I needed a Zeebe fix. Zaonna excitedly agreed with my proposal and stood tall in her new title as mom.

My house seemed unusually quiet, my heart unashamedly sad. I focused my energy on rehearsing the positives and practicality of this decision. At times that was helpful. But at other times I didn't care what made sense. I just craved holding her, feeding her, and cuddling with that precious bundle of purring joy. The only thing left to do was place Zeebe in God's care and find comfort in knowing at least someone's heart was singing.

~~~

The memories of six weeks before faded and the garage door opened. I drove in mechanically and closed it behind me. Turning off the car jolted me back to reality and my mind cleared. Suddenly everything made sense. Of course! This little family I had just met in my garden was Zeebe's family! The two tiny kittens Jeff had found in the shop six weeks before were two of three siblings. My new garden friend had to be Zeebe's sister, the coat colors and markings were a remarkable match. The black kitten had to be the one mama cat reclaimed in the shed. How could I not have realized that sooner? I couldn't wait to tell everyone.

Now, more than ever, I longed to rescue Zeebe's sister. It was obvious that this mama cat had chosen the black one as her favorite and didn't care much for the zebra-striped pair. She had abandoned one in the shed and seemed to scorn the other. How sad was that? I vowed to win the trust of my new friend as quickly as possible.

Where has this little family been for the last six weeks? Why have I not seen them before? How have they survived?

Early the next morning I was off to check on the little family. The light from the doorway exposed the empty food bowl on the dirt floor. The water bowl had been used. *They ate the food and drank the water. Hallelujah! They are here. My plan might work after all.*

I began calling for the little bundle of energy. "Here kitty, kitty. I'm back. Where are you? I have some more food for you. Kitty, kitty. I have some great news for you. I know where your long-lost sister is—the one you wouldn't remember because you were only a day old when you got separated." I walked around the garden and into the field. "I have a name for you, little one. It matches your sister's. I'm going to call you Zeeba in honor of your beautiful stripes. Here Zeeba. Here kitty, kitty."

I scanned the field for any sign of movement. Nothing. *This is not going to be as easy as I thought. It's going to take a lot of time and patience. God help me.* I made the decision right then to do whatever it took to win Zeeba's trust and one day claim her as my own. Little did I know the energy, time, and patience this commitment would require.

Every day I checked the bowls, found them emptied, and replenished them. But nowhere could I find the hungry recipients of the food and water gifts.

"Zeeba! Where are you? Kitty, kitty." The enthusiasm in my voice was dwindling. "Here little family. Where are you hiding?"

What can I do? They must come back only at night to eat, and then go somewhere else during the day. Where would they go? Maybe they are still sleeping when I come in the morning. Perhaps I can catch them later in the day. I decided to try visiting at different times during the day.

That plan didn't prove successful. Then I had a creative idea. *What if I don't leave food for them at night but come in the morning to feed them? They would surely be hungry and maybe that hunger would override their fear. What a great idea, Sheila! That way they will also get used to being around you.*

I arrived early the next morning and opened the shed door as wide as it would go. As I walked in, I called for my vagrant family.

"Here kitty, kitty. Zeeba! Zeeba! Come get some breakfast. Come, little family. I have some food and water for you."

I couldn't believe my ears. Little meows and rustling drifted down from above me. *You've got to be kidding! That mom has those kittens in the attic?* I poured food in the dish and hoped the sound would motivate a showing. The meows continued but no faces appeared. *Let's see what happens if I leave the shed.*

I stood outside for a few minutes waiting. To my delight, I opened the door again to see three bodies around the food dish. Two of them vanished immediately but Zeeba retreated to the corner of the shed to survey her domain. I stood by the door to give her more room and began talking softly to her. Keeping her eye on me, she gingerly advanced toward the food. She positioned herself so she could see me and eat at the same time. This became a daily ritual for us. Every few days, however, I moved a step closer to the bowl and remained still while she ate. One day I stood close enough to reach out my arm and touch her, but I didn't dare. A few days later I stood close to the bowl, placing my foot on the edge. She remained guarded and any movement I made frightened her. *Patience, Sheila, patience.*

In addition to the feeding process, Zeeba and I began meeting in the garden as well. She would prance in circles around me as I talked to her and begged her to let me pet her. It seemed she wanted the affection as much as I wanted to give it, but fear kept distance between us. When she appeared, I would slowly make my way to a grassy area and sit down. She would rub up against sticks and rocks—anything she could—while she purred and padded the ground. When she would come within reach, I wanted so badly to grab her and hold her tight. I wanted her to experience my loving touch and know I was safe.

But I knew better. Grabbing her and holding her would negate the budding trust. I reminded myself that there is nothing about love that is forced. Real love is by invitation only, and one must have total freedom to accept or reject it. I didn't want to spoil my chances of one day winning her complete trust, so I remained still. I used my voice, instead, to pet her and invite her. I must have told her a million times how much I loved her and wanted to hold her and take her home with me. She listened and flirted often with the idea of coming to me but remained elusive.

I will never forget the first day I finally got to touch her. I had been squatting down beside the food bowl and placing my hand on the bowl while she ate. I had reached over to her a couple of times and she had backed away. But this time, she allowed me to touch her little head. I could see her body stiffen, but she continued to eat. She must have been exceptionally hungry. The next day she let me pet her a couple times on her head, and the next day her tiny back. A few days later she began purring as I carefully stroked her. "Oh Zeeba," I cried softly. "You are so adorable. I have been waiting forever for this day. I can't wait to hold you!"

That afternoon in the garden, she rubbed up against my shoe for the first time. I held out my hand. "Zeeba, I want to hold you so much.

When are you ever going to let me hold you? I'm so excited you are beginning to trust me more. I understand trust takes time. And that's OK, sweetie. You take all the time you need." I heard my calm voice but it did not match the anxious feelings inside. It had been a month and a half since I met her in July and we still had a long way to go before I could bring her home. August was going by fast and the weather was beginning to cool. My goal was to have her home before winter set in.

Zeeba must have heard my anxious heart. She began coming to me and allowing me to pet her. I sat on an upside down five-gallon bucket each day as she ate. When she finished, she would come and rub against my leg. Once, she let me pick her up for a second and put her on my lap to pet her. She instantly jumped down and ran off, but gradually, each day, she stayed in my lap longer.

When I called for her now, she would come immediately from places on our property. Her mom and brother always kept their distance and would never come and eat when I was there. Whenever Zeeba would run to her mom for attention, she was always rejected. Her mom would move to avoid her or bat her away and run off. My heart ached for her. I had to figure out a way to step up this trust-building process.

The next step, I figured, was getting her used to my car. I didn't want her to be afraid when I took her home in it. I slowly drove it closer to the shed, opened the car door, and started calling her.

"Zeeba, Zeeba. Come here, kitty. Come explore mommy's car." My arm was stretched out to pet her on the ground as we talked. "This is the car you will ride in when I take you home with me. You need to get used to it, sweetie." She sniffed all the way around the car but couldn't find the courage to jump inside. "You are very curious, little one, aren't you? It won't hurt you. I promise."

A couple of days later, after much coaxing, she jumped in my lap and then proceeded to explore every inch of the interior of my car, including the top of the dashboard and the backseat window shelf. For the next few days, we played and talked and cuddled. When I felt she was sufficiently relaxed inside the car, I decided to risk the next step— starting the engine. It's a good thing I had the door open because she couldn't get out fast enough! With new scratches and worries, I headed home. I was afraid I had permanently ruined her car experience.

Happily, she wasn't too terrified to return to the car the next day. "Well, hello, Zeeba. I'm so excited to see you. I was worried you would be afraid and stay away from my car. You are so precious to forgive me so quickly for yesterday's scare." Zeeba curled up in my lap and purred even louder as if to confirm her forgiveness. "I know you won't like it, sweetie, but I must keep trying until you get accustomed to the engine noise. I wish you could understand. I hope that soon you will trust me completely and somehow know that I have your best interest in mind— always."

Once I could start the car with her in it and she would stay put, we advanced to getting used to having the door shut, and then attempting to drive around a bit. She hated being inside with the car moving, so I didn't push it. I reasoned that when the time came, she could bear the trauma for the short ride home. For now, I wouldn't subject her to any more riding since that would be a rare part of her life with humans.

It was time to introduce her to Jeff, her new daddy-to-be, and see if she would accept him in her space. Jeff came with me to the shop the next day. I was in for a shocking surprise.

"Zeeba, I've brought you a new friend today. Look who is here to meet you." She bounded in the door and I closed it behind her. I wanted to make sure she would stay in the shop and get used to his smell and his voice without running off.

Jeff sat down on my usual bucket seat on the floor of the shop. I knelt close to him and we both talked to her as I petted her on the floor beside us. To my utter amazement, she didn't seem alarmed by his voice and even allowed him to pet her that very first day.

"That's not fair," I whined. I've had to work so hard just to get to this point and you walk right in and get to enjoy her immediately." I consoled myself with the truth that all my work and patience is what made this possible. Because of the trust she had in me, she could trust him. I accepted the compliment and stopped whining.

The next day she allowed Jeff to pick her up and pet her in his lap. She enjoyed his attention just as much, or more, than mine. "Well, I'll be, Zeeba. How quickly you accept this stranger into your life. It must be because you don't have a daddy? At least, I've never seen one around. Now you have one. His name is Jeff and he will love you as much as I do. You are blessed, little Zeeba."

Friday morning the announcer on the radio wished me a happy first day of fall. Instantly, I felt a sense of urgency for Zeeba. *What more do I need to do before I can bring her home? I know she drinks water and eats food. She seems great with Jeff. What else?* I began planning how this transition was going to play out. I'd bring her home and then keep her inside for a few days or weeks until I felt she was comfortable in her new home. That thought introduced a necessary step I had overlooked. There would be no dirt or garden in our home. She had to learn to use a cat box! *Oh dear. How am I going to do this?*

Eventually, I came up with a plan to lock her inside the shop for a few days to see if she would use a cat box. It seemed cruel, but I couldn't think of a better way.

Off to the store I went to buy cat litter and a pan. When I returned, she happily followed me into the shop and playfully batted at the cat litter as I poured it into the pan.

"This is your new outhouse, Zeeba. It's a replacement for dirt when you are inside our home. And there are benefits. See, your adorable paws won't get dirty. They'll stay nice and clean. Isn't that wonderful?"

I put her in it a couple of times and showed her how to scratch and dig holes. I wondered how mommy cats taught their babies how to dig holes, use them, and then cover up their messes. Perhaps just modeling it was enough. I laughed out loud just thinking about it. "No, this mommy won't be modeling that for you. If mama cat didn't teach you already, you're going to have to learn some other way." She looked at me as if I were crazy. I laugh a lot, but this was the first time she had heard me.

"Zeeba, I hope your mom taught you how to cover up when you go. I'm anxious to see if you will use this. Before you can come home with me, I must know you can. That's the only reason I'm going to leave you in the shop for a while. I'm so sorry to do this to you. I'll be back often so you don't need to be afraid. And here's a little box and blanket for you to sleep in. I know this will be hard for you to understand. You are my wild kitty, and outdoors *is* home. But I don't know any other way to find out if you can survive in our home, at least until I can begin letting you outside. Please forgive me, sweetie."

With my hand on the doorknob, I leaned down and petted her one more time. Brushing a tear away, I exited and quickly closed the door behind me. I thought about challenges in my own life that I didn't understand and about how hard it is to trust that the One who knows me best, knows what's best for me. *God, please help little Zeeba to learn quickly and not be afraid.*

Early the next morning, I drove to the shop. I couldn't wait to see if Zeeba was OK and if she had used the litter box. I was praying she had because the alternative would require cleaning up any messes, and that was *not* my idea of fun.

"Zeeba, we're back. Daddy and mommy are here. Where are you?" She crawled out from under the car looking rather sleepy. It didn't take her any time at all, though, to find her voice as I opened some cat food for her.

"How did you do, sweetie? Were you OK being alone in here? Were you able to use your new dirt?" I glanced over at the box and it looked as if she had been in it. *I wonder if she did more than play in it?* Nothing was visible, so either she was just playing in it or she *did* know how to cover things up. We began sifting through the litter with the scoop.

"You are amazing, Zeeba. Wow! What a good kitty you are. You even covered everything up. I'm so proud of you!" She seemed delighted we were there and happily soaked up the double portion of affection. She rubbed up against our legs, jumped into our laps and then down, and circled around and around as we petted her. It seemed she couldn't get enough.

"Honey, do you think she's ready to come home?"

"I wouldn't be too hasty, Sheila. This seems too easy. It's hard to believe she could make that transition so quickly."

We searched the shop floor to make sure there were no messes anywhere else. It astonished and thrilled us when we came up with nothing.

"I know you're excited to bring her home, but I think it would be wise to wait a couple more days to be sure."

That was Wednesday. Thursday was the same. Friday, I woke up with an unshakable longing to bring her home. I didn't want to wait one more day. Besides, we would be home more over the weekend to help her adapt. She had proven she could take care of herself and be away from her family. It was time.

"What do you think, Jeff? I'm thinking it's time to bring Zeeba home? We'll both be home this weekend and can spend more time with her to help her adjust."

"I don't know why not. She's using her box and she seems to be comfortable with us. I think she's ready." I could tell he was smitten with Zeeba love too.

My heart was singing as I drove home after work. I pulled my car up close to the shop and opened the shop door. She came running. I picked her up and held her close.

"Are you ready to come home with me, Zeeba?"

She looked at me so curiously, as if she knew something was up. I sat down and cuddled with her for a few minutes. She seemed so content; I hated to spoil her contentment with the stressful ride home. I knew the change would be traumatic for her and getting familiar with a new place overwhelming. I resolved to make this as quick and painless as possible for her.

I began picking up her bowls, food, litter box, and bed and taking them to the car. She was eager to get outside every time I opened the door, but I was afraid she would run away, and I wouldn't be able to get her back. The sun was setting, and I wouldn't have time to spend coaxing her to the car. Finally, the car was loaded, and it was time to take Zeeba on her first wild ride.

I picked her up and wrapped her in my arms. "Today is the day, Zeeba. I can't wait for you to see your new home. You will love it. It is much bigger than this shop and there is no mean mama cat around. Just two big people who love and adore you!"

Opening the car door, I felt her body tense. "We have to go in the car, Zeeba, to your new home. It's going to be OK—you'll see. I'll drive very carefully. Life is going to be amazing for you in your new place." Her little heart was beating fast, and I was sure she hadn't heard one word I said. I tried to calm her before starting the car, but she was not willing.

She frantically ran all over the car. All I could do was talk to her and try to reassure her. "We're almost there, honey. See, there is your new house. I'm opening the garage door and driving in. You are going to be just fine."

The garage door closed behind us and I quickly opened the car door to let her escape. Jumping out was good and bad. She was glad to be free but was not expecting all the new smells and unknown territory.

"Come inside, Zeeba. Let me introduce you to your new home. I'm so excited you are finally here!"

Jeff came upstairs and joined in the process of acquainting Zeeba with her new space. She calmed down and allowed Jeff to hold her for a few minutes as we sat on the sofa. Soon she was off again to do more exploring.

By now the sun was hiding behind the mountain and the edges of the gray clouds were turning pink. Jeff announced, "It looks like a storm is coming in."

"Oh no! That won't be fun for Zeeba. A storm the first night she is home? She's going to think this new place is a scary place to be."

Sure enough. We stood watching as bolts of lightning ripped the dark sky. Then the thunder added its booming special effects. Zeeba didn't stay around to admire the storm but ran for cover. I found her crouched under a chair by the window.

"Oh honey, come here, little one. Let me take you away from this noise. You are right by the window where it is the loudest."

I scooped her up and took her to the other side of the house away from the windows. I fixed her bed in the laundry room next to her litter box. She wasn't impressed. Her eyes were huge and she kept running back under the chair by the window. I was so sad and worried that this would make her transition way more difficult. I settled on the floor by the chair and kept talking to her and petting her.

The storm eventually passed, and all was quiet. She came out from under the chair and finally calmed down enough to eat a few bites before we retreated to bed.

"Oh, Zeeba. I'm so sorry for this dreadful initiation to our home. It really is rare to see such an intense storm. Most of the time it's peaceful and quiet. You'll see. For now, I'm just so thankful it's over." I curled up beside her bed and stroked her head and back. Those precious little eyes finally closed, her body relaxed, and the purring faded. *Thank you, God, for the calm after the storm.* I took advantage of the quiet, kissed sleeping beauty good-night, and headed for bed.

She was back to normal the next morning and eager to face the world again. We thoroughly enjoyed holding her, playing with her, feeding her, and watching as she explored her new home.

After two weeks of indoor living, I introduced Zeeba to our lawn and her new outdoor surroundings. Each day we would spend a little more time outside and I would give her more and more freedom to roam about. She soon reconnected with her passion for the outdoors, growing less and less content with the indoors. The windows and doors occupied her time where she grandstanded her preference.

We quickly advanced from playful outings on the lawn to frisky expeditions in the wooded area close to the house. We played tag and catch-me-if-you-can games on the little path that winds through the woods to a beautiful park. Hard as I tried, she was always the declared winner.

Her fascination with all the trees, bushes, and tall grass was understandable. It was a very different world than the barren, weed-infested field where she grew up. This playground had her name all over it; I'm sure she thought it was heaven.

Sometimes Zeebe's family would come and visit. Zaonna, Doronna, and Zjé loved Zeeba too. We dreamed of getting the two siblings together someday and wished they wouldn't grow up so fast.

Most of all, we were so grateful for the love and entertainment both kittens had brought into our lives.

Zeeba seemed to transition from kitten to cat instantaneously. She flew past any awkward growing-up years and immediately adopted an adult stance with come-and-go privileges. She reversed our roles with zero regard for my needs or approval. Now her time indoors was at her discretion, and the amount of time spent was reduced from hours to minutes. She had a two-part goal in mind when she came meowing to the door: food and love. As soon as she got her fill, she would jump down and trot to the door where she sat impatiently vocalizing her demand to be released into her world.

Her favorite pastime became hunting. Not casual play hunting, but *hunting*. Anything that moved was fair game—mice, squirrels, rabbits, garter snakes, and all kinds of birds that made their home in "her" territory were seriously at risk. The worst part of it was when she proudly brought me each conquest. I couldn't bring myself to congratulate her. Instead, I'd run the other way, begging Jeff to come and take the gift away, please.

Occasionally, something good would happen with her live catch. When she brought it up on the deck, she made an eerie, guttural meow announcing her victory and arrival. When I heard that awful sound, I would run outside to meet her, not to affirm her, but to try and save the victim. Often the bird was still alive and if I yelled loud enough, Zeeba opened her mouth and the bird flew away. As far as birds are concerned, nothing brought me greater joy than to free them.

Poor Zeeba. She didn't understand my ungrateful behavior. To her credit, though, she refused to spend much time brooding over her loss. Instead, she would run off in search of another challenge.

Between hunting adventures, Zeeba began developing a strange behavior that took me awhile to decipher. She would wait patiently outside my sliding door, and when I would open it, she would scamper across the deck or dart around the corner toward the spiral staircase. It seemed like a flirty invitation to play, and sometimes I would chase her for a bit on the deck, thinking that is what she wanted. But playing games didn't seem to interest her, leaving me bewildered. When I would go back inside, she would come again to the door, wait, and then tear off again when I opened it.

I began noticing out my window that she would sit at the top of the stairs and keep looking back toward the door. *What in the world do you want, Zeeba? If you don't want to play, what do you want?*

What she wanted was for me to follow her. Duh. I slipped on some shoes in preparation for following wherever she led. Sure enough, her mood changed drastically, and she flashed the biggest cat grin I'd ever seen.

"Where do you want to go, Zeeba?" Off she ran to the bottom of the stairs and waited there for me. When I got down the stairs, she ran around the pool toward the back lawn and waited there. Each time I caught up to her, she would run a little farther. Finally, she took me all the way down to the end of our lawn by the river. Black locust trees lined the riverbank and provided tall scratching posts and bark-covered vertical bars for her gymnastic stunts. And did she ever put on a show. She would race up the trunk, then jump down and race up the next tree. In an instant, she would leap back to my side where she would briefly allow a few pets, then race off again. Her heart was beating so fast; she seemed delirious. Her excitement about having me in her world was unmistakable.

Finally, she settled down and we lay side by side, eye to eye on the soft grass. She serenaded me with her purring while I massaged her head and ears and neck and back. It was our little love nest.

When it came time for me to go back inside, I started climbing up our sloping lawn thinking she would follow me. I glanced back and was surprised to see she hadn't moved. She looked so forlorn. The grin had vanished, and she sat perfectly still, stubbornly protesting my retreat.

"Come on, Zeeba." I pleaded. "I'm not abandoning you. It's time to go in. I can't stay out here all night, sweetie." No response. She just sat there staring into space. Defiant. No amount of coaxing could change her mind. I walked to the bottom of the stairs leading to the pool, up the stairs, around the pool, up the spiral stairs, around the corner to my bedroom door and turned to look again. There she sat.

"Zeeba. Here kitty, kitty. I'll give you some yummy food. Come on, sweetie. We'll go again soon, I promise." Not even a twitch. *Wow. This cat has mastered the silent treatment. She is a serious punisher when she doesn't get her way.* I laughed to myself and slipped into the bedroom. As soon as she heard the door sliding shut, she relinquished her frozen state and bounded down the path toward the woods.

That day marked the beginning of a routine for us. Her shameless begging for it far outweighed my time for it. Her consuming daily desire, it seemed, was for me to come away from my world and enter hers.

One day, as I lay on the grass beside her in our usual spot by the river, I had a revelation. Zeeba and I had come full circle. I had met her in the wild, coaxed her ever so gently and lovingly into my world. She had rewarded my unconditional love and pursuit with trust and a willingness to join my world. Then she encountered the gigantic, beautiful, green, and woodsy world around us and made it her kingdom. Because she was torn between both worlds, she came up with a plan to try and coax me into coming and living in the wild with her. With patience and tireless pursuit, she lovingly invited me to join her world time and time again. And when my world got especially crazy, and we shared a peace and love by the river, I was tempted. But not for long. All I had to do was consider her diet and the temptation vanished.

Sorry, Zeeba. Not in this earthly world. I'll come and visit your world, just as you come and visit mine, but we'll have to agree to be content, for now, with our love that bridges and enhances both our worlds. Together we can dream of the world to come with a perfect garden that will surpass our wildest imaginations and dreams, a garden we both will be proud to call home.

~~~

From wild to tame, our Zeeba came;

Back to wild she returned, never the same.

She found a love stronger than fear,

A trust that helped her see her way clear.

She discovered a world she never dreamed of

And an adoring family that she could love.

She enjoys the best of both worlds today,

But longs to live fully together, someday.

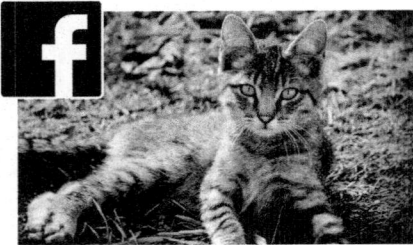

For more information and upcoming books from Sheila Schroeder, go to:
SheilaSchroeder.com

For books coming soon from After the Rain Publishing LLC, visit:
AftertheRainPublishing.com

After the Rain
Publishing LLC

barcode

CPSIA information can be obtained
at www.ICGtesting.com
Printed in the USA
LVOW13s1243280318
571444LV00008B/45/P

9 780999 681237